Music Minus One 'Cello

3716

ETHAN WINER
Concerto for Cello & Orchestra in A minor

FRANZ SCHUBERT
Ave Maria

SAINT-SAËNS
Allegro Appassionato

Printed in Canada

MMO CD 3716

Music Minus One

WINER: Concerto for Cello & Orchestra in A minor

Complete	Background Track	Title	Page No.
1	5	*Ethan Winer:* Cello Concerto in A minor	5
	6	Cello Entrance	
2	7	*Franz Schubert:* Ave Maria	11
3	8	*Saint Saëns:* "Insaen" pop version of Allegro Appassionato	12
4		-Tuning Notes, A440-	

Steven Thomas *Charcoal drawing by Glaucia Prado-Thomas drawn at the recording session.*

Concerto for 'Cello and Orchestra in A minor

(in one movement)

Solo Cello

by Ethan Winer

Allegro Moderato ♩= 104

Cadenza (approx. 2:25)

Concerto Performance Notes:

I have tried to make my intent for fingerings and phrasing as clear as possible in the printed music, including alternate fingerings where appropriate. A few additional points are worth noting.

1) In several places there are notes with legato lines that not only should be played longer than normal, but also should begin slightly early to give an added emphasis. The pickup note into section "C" is one such example, as are the pickups to "I" and "P" and the entrance at "D."

2) The 8va option in section "G" is much higher than the clarinet line that precedes it, but if you can pull it off, it should sound terrific in that register.

3) The Animato section starting at "T" should be played as fast you can reasonably handle, in much the same spirit as the third movement of the Haydn C Major concerto. The orchestra is pretty much coasting there, though bear in mind that the solo oboe doubles the cello in "U" and must be able to keep up.

4) There are two places in the cadenza that a slight pause will give a nice added emphasis just before the changes in tonality. One place is the G# in measure 30, which should be held a bit longer than normal. The other is the middle of measure 43, where you could hold the G slightly before playing the Ab that follows.

Ave Maria

by F.Schubert

Allegro Appassionato

by Camille Saint-Saëns

14

legg

dimin.

poco meno mosso.

dolce.

a tempo.

cresc.

p

f

ff

15

In the Express Lane: Learning the Cello as an Adult

by Ethan Winer

I began playing the cello at the age of 43, and at the time considered myself fortunate to undertake this admittedly large project as an adult. As an adult I didn't have to contend with the trauma of outgrowing an instrument. I'd also played other instruments (electric guitar, Fender bass, some piano), and already understood how music "works." Perhaps most important, I had a determination to succeed that few children possess.

But starting as an adult also has unique drawbacks. Playing endless variations of "Twinkle Twinkle Little Star" is hardly interesting to someone who's studied musical scores and performed publicly. Worse, I knew how good music is supposed to be played, and my early efforts were not even close. Beginner children don't know how bad they sound, and thus are not so easily discouraged! Having played blues lead guitar for many years I knew what it felt like to be in control of an instrument--to play with feeling and conviction. I really hated being demoted to mediocre status as a beginner on the cello, and wanted to get past that phase as quickly as possible. What I hoped would be an enjoyable pastime soon evolved into an obsession to become proficient as quickly as possible that now occupies three or four hours of each day.

In the five years since I began playing the cello I've made a number of observations that I believe other adult beginners and intermediate players--especially those who are ambitious and are willing to work hard--will find useful. Like Sergeant Joe Friday on the TV show Dragnet, I have always been a seeker of "just the facts." I'm not interested in guesses, half-baked opinions, or anything that can't be substantiated. The facts I wanted to know are 1) What skills are needed to become an accomplished cellist, and 2) How do I get there in the shortest amount of time?

In a previous career I owned a software company, and wrote books and magazine articles about computer programming. Being a successful programmer requires knowing the facts, and learning to play an instrument really is no different. However, to become a proficient player requires learning the facts *and also* developing the necessary mechanical skills. A good musician possesses "fine motor control" as well as the artistic sense to know how to apply that control.

I'm convinced that what is often mistaken for musical talent or aptitude is really persistence and enough belief in one's self to keep at it. It takes thousands of practice hours to achieve competence and even more to become truly polished. Unfortunately, many people give up long before then, mistakenly believing they don't have the needed ability. But like walking and talking, most of the skills necessary for playing an instrument are purely mechanical and can be developed by anyone given enough time. How one actually applies that mechanical, muscular control is what distinguishes the truly talented from the merely competent.

WHAT YOUR TEACHER WON'T TELL YOU

Most of my studying has been with one teacher, to whom I remain devoted. But I've also taken single lessons from a number of other teachers, to get additional opinions and to hear as many different viewpoints as possible. The more my understanding of the cello has grown, the more surprised I am that few of these teachers addressed certain mechanical aspects of playing the cello--in particular, the importance and difficulty of the bow.

Many professional cellists and teachers achieve a beautiful tone, yet cannot describe what it is they do physically to get that tone. I've been told, "Draw the sound out, don't push it inward," which conveys no information and provides no guidance for how to do that! Likewise, comments such as "Make a big sound" and "Play with more resonance" are equally useless. Resonance is a physical property (a propensity to vibrate), not something that a player controls. And a good cellist can make a "big sound" even when playing very softly. In the pursuit of a beautiful tone, bowing is the single most important skill to master. Bowing is the cello's voice, and everything else revolves around that.

Bowing an instrument is an inherently awkward act. It is easy for a teacher who has been playing since an early age to overlook the amount of strength and control needed just to draw the bow smoothly. What happens in the first few milliseconds of a note has an enormous bearing on the perceived character of the entire note. A scratchy tone or flat pitch caused by too fast or too slow a bow speed--even if corrected quickly--will make the entire note or passage sound amateurish. Controlling a bow and changing its direction are some of the most difficult things to master, yet smooth bow changes are fundamental to playing the cello. Until you can change bow direction without making a scratching sound, every note you play will sound lame. If you listen to a recording of any great cellist playing a slow passage you will note that every bow change is flawless and beautiful--all you hear at each note transition is the slightest dip in volume.

Note initiations can be sudden with a biting effect, or they can be gentle followed by a gradual increase in volume. But a biting start should never be distorted or scratchy. Cello strings are thick and heavy, and it takes a lot of strength to get them moving. But pressing even a little too hard or drawing the bow even a little too fast ruins the sound. Even more difficult is changing bow direction while also changing the bow to a different string. These are the things a beginner must focus on the most to overcome sounding like a beginner.

Another obstacle is developing an independence of the left and right arms and hands. Not unlike the joke about walking and chewing gum at the same time, it is harder to move your left hand accurately on the fingerboard while also changing the bow direction. I've theorized that the brain splits its concentration between the two hands, making it harder to control the bow and the left hand fingers at the same time. There are difficult passages I can play confidently and in tune using pizzicato, but that are weak and out of tune when played with the bow. Likewise, I can do a smoother bow change if I first stop the vibrato. I know in time bowing will become automatic, and at that point I'll work at continuing vibrato up to the exact moment when a new note begins.

Finally, many teachers stress that you should remain relaxed when you play. But how can you possibly relax as you approach a passage you know you have only a small chance of playing well? The fact is you can't! By all means try to relax--in my case I tend to grip the bow too tightly in a vain effort to gain control--but also accept that you won't become fully comfortable until you've been playing for many years.

PRACTICE SMARTER, NOT HARDER

I won't dispute the value of conventional learning methods--studying etude books and progressively more difficult student pieces--but I'm convinced there's an even faster way to become a competent cellist. It's been said that a month of on-the-job training is equal to a year of college. By extension, you will progress faster by working on real pieces rather than etudes and student compositions. Further, if you practice etudes for three years, all you have to show for your effort is, well, etudes. However, if you start now on a real concerto or sonata, you'll have learned and be able to play a beautiful and meaningful piece of music for the same amount of effort. But you also need to develop mechanical facility.

My practice hours are divided about equally between works from the standard cello literature and highly focused mechanical exercises. It is these exercises that I want to share here, and I'm convinced they are more useful than an etude book for a motivated adult student. I have practiced these exercises daily for five years now, and I can attest that they work and work well. By focusing directly on the most difficult mechanical aspects of cello playing, you can reduce what might otherwise take ten or more years to substantially less than that. After mastering the mechanics you can then work on the more artistic aspects of this noble craft.

In the pursuit of a clear tone, the Number One issue is achieving the ideal ratio of these three interrelated factors: bow speed, bow pressure, and bow distance from the bridge. As the bow is drawn faster, more pressure is required to maintain the optimum amount of friction. It is this optimum friction that makes for a "big" sound. Cellists sometimes use less bow pressure or more speed to get a beautiful silky tone, which can be enhanced by placing the bow farther from the bridge. A special effect called Sul Ponticello uses a similar technique with the bow placed very close to the bridge. But first you must develop the bow control needed to create a clear tone--what I call a "pure buzz."

If the bow moves too fast at the start of a note it creates a scratching sound; on sustained notes too much speed or too little pressure makes the bow skate over the string instead of digging into it. When the bow speed is too slow or the pressure is too great the note becomes distorted, or even flat in pitch. Likewise, when the bow is nearer to the bridge more pressure is needed or, alternatively, the bow must be drawn more slowly. This is especially apparent when playing fast passages on the lower strings when changing bow direction for each note. Different notes--even on the same string--also have a different optimum speed for a given amount of pressure. As you play the short example in Figure 1 (all on the G string), notice how difficult it is to prevent a brief scratching sound as each new note begins.

Figure 1

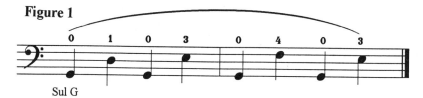

Sul G

Achieving the optimum ratio of speed and pressure is hardest when bowing near to the bridge, due to the very slow speed needed to sound a clear tone. It's hard to keep such a slow speed steady. Yet this is where a soloist must play during loud passages, to rise above the rest of the orchestra. It is harder still to bow slowly very near the frog end.

I practice three similar exercises to develop the control needed to smoothly change bow direction and maintain a pure tone during slow passages. The first exercise is simply drawing the bow back and forth on each string twenty times, trying to avoid a scratching sound when the bow changes direction. The scratching is caused by the bow traveling too quickly, and these exercises force you to work at reducing the speed. Place the bow within an inch of the bridge and an inch from the frog, and draw about two inches of bow in each direction keeping the bow in contact with the string at all times. The other two exercises shown in Figures 2a and 2b are variations that help develop smooth bow crossings. Do each of these exercises as cleanly as possible on each string pair bowing near the frog, starting both down- and up-bow, at least 20 times every day.

Figure 2a

Figure 2b

Equally valuable is practicing slow scales, always drawing the bow fully from one end to the other. It is tempting to avoid the last few inches at each end of the bow, but I urge you not to. If something is hard to do or uncomfortable, that's a sure sign you need to practice it! Again, try to achieve a pure buzz, with no scuffing sound when the bow direction changes. Also practice drawing the bow on each string as slowly as possible, sustaining a single bow in each direction for at least 30 seconds or longer and as smoothly as possible. This is easiest to do when the bow is farther away from the bridge. Baseball players develop strength and control by swinging two bats at once. In a similar manner, trying to bow more slowly than you'll ever really need expedites developing a steady bow arm. The secret of making a powerful tone at low volumes is keeping the bow very steady. It is the slight fluctuations in bow speed and pressure that make a note sound wimpy, like it's played by a beginner.

Another useful exercise is what I call "touch downs," which help develop the ability to drop the bow onto a string without it bouncing. This is especially difficult to do near the tip of the bow. Starting at the frog end of the bow about a half inch above the C string, lower the bow slowly and carefully, draw one inch of bow, raise it, back up a half inch, and repeat until you have reached the tip. Do that once again working toward the frog, and then repeat on the other strings. (I joke to my friends that I spend half my practice time trying to keep the bow from bouncing when I don't want it to, and the other half trying to get it to bounce when it won't.)

Also valuable are what I think of as the bowing equivalents to tongue twisters--exercises that for one reason or another are more difficult than they might appear on a printed page. Changing the bow direction while also going to a different string is more difficult than staying on the same string. By focusing on bowing exercises that demand this movement you will practice the needed moves more often than they would occur in a normal piece or etude. These are shown in Figures 3a through 3e.

Figure 3a

Figure 3b

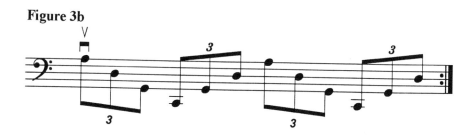

Figure 3c

(play each measure 4 times)

Figure 3d

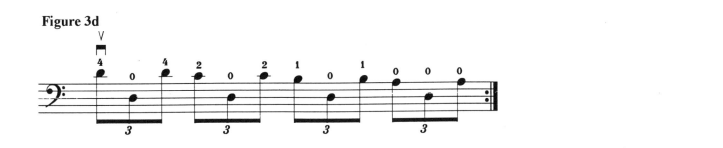

Figure 3e

I spend a few minutes every day on each of these exercises, going as slowly as necessary to sound each note clearly and not accidentally hit two strings at once. Then I do them again as fast as possible, ignoring that the bow doesn't dig optimally into the strings, to get my hands used to "making the motions" quickly and smoothly. Do the exercises in Figures 3d and 3e starting both down- and up-bow, and also on every string-pair.

The exercises in 4a and 4b are also harder to play than they look because the fingering itself is tricky. Figure 4c is a real challenge to play in tune because it leads with the fourth finger descending instead of the first finger which is more usual. Push yourself to play these as quickly as possible, but without making a jumble of the notes.

Figure 4a

Figure 4b

Sul A (practice both fingerings shown)

Figure 4c

Sul A

Besides the difficulty of mastering string crossings, it is a challenge just to coordinate bowing and fingering. The tried and true exercises in Figures 5a and 5b will be useful to players at any skill level; you can never play them fast enough or cleanly enough. Again, do them starting both down- and up-bow, and first slowly and then quickly. Also do the exercise in Figure 5a in the key of D (a whole step higher) to get your left hand fingers used to the large stretches needed to play in that key in first position.

Figure 5a

All in first position

Figure 5b

All in first position

All in first position

Bowing is important, but so are smooth position shifts. The exercise in Figure 6 is meant to be played all on the G string, but you should also repeat it on the other strings. At each shift point try to make the shift as smoothly as possible--never sudden or jerky. If you're not sure how to shift positions smoothly ask your teacher to show you. There's a special way to do that which is not necessarily obvious. Go up and down each string at least eight times, and you'll be amazed at how soon you are comfortable playing near the very top of the fingerboard.

Figure 6

I also urge you to explore thumb position if you haven't already, and practice scales and arpeggios daily that extend to the highest positions on the neck. Playing a four-octave arpeggio is not something you'll be able to do all of a sudden one day "when you are good." You have to start sometime, so why not today? Go as slowly as necessary to start, and don't be discouraged by how slowly you have to play to stay in tune.

Finally, make up your own exercises based on pieces you find difficult to play. There are many other bowing and fingering exercises not shown here that I practice every day, and many were derived from one passage or another that I stumbled over during the course of playing real pieces. For example, when I had trouble playing this phrase from the Dvorak Concerto (Figure 7):

Figure 7

I made up the exercise shown in Figure 8 and added it to my daily to-do list.

Figure 8

For an additional challenge, use the second left hand finger instead of the third for the high note in the middle of each figure. Then do it again using the first finger each time for that high note. This exercise is especially useful because it requires shifting repeatedly over the awkward area where the neck joins the body of the cello.

BEYOND EXERCISES

Mechanical exercises are valuable because they focus on specific aspects of cello technique. They are admittedly boring, but the work must be done. However, exercises won't help you with sight reading, or further your understanding of musical concepts. The best way to improve your reading skills is to keep working on new pieces. Try to find a local orchestra to play with, or start a piano trio or string quartet. It's difficult to find advanced players willing to practice with a beginner, but at least try to find others who are as dedicated as you so you won't outgrow them. Many towns have a community orchestra you can join even if you are not that advanced. Play the passages you can, and rest or play softly during the hard parts. Or play only the first note in each group of four sixteenth notes. Nobody will mind if you can't play everything perfectly, as long as you don't wreck it for the others by playing out of tune too loudly. Joining an amateur orchestra has the added benefit of sitting beside someone more experienced who can show you fingerings and other techniques. After struggling for several months to learn spiccato, a cellist in a local group showed me the basic moves in five minutes during coffee break.

Equally valuable is attending concerts and watching video tapes. I have most of the cello videos available, and I've learned something useful from every one of them. The Shar catalog (800-248-SHAR) lists a number of videos--both teaching and complete performances--and for about the cost of an hour-long lesson they're a good value. I've also bought all of the cello CDs offered by Music Minus One (914-592-1188). The only minor problem with accompaniment CDs is they are played at full tempo, which sometimes is too fast for a beginner. But nothing beats playing along with superb musicians who get it right every time. I've also created my own accompaniments in my home MIDI recording studio, which has the advantage of letting me vary the playback tempo over a very wide range without altering the pitch of the instruments.

AL FINE

If you watch an expert cellist playing a difficult piece, it is tempting to think, "That must be very hard to do." But obviously it is not hard for that cellist! I have a wise friend who once pointed out "It's only hard if you can't do it." Becoming good enough to perform an advanced piece with ease is what's difficult. Playing any instrument is a lifetime commitment, and the best cellists are those who continue to practice their craft every day.

Ethan Winer, 1997

Notes on the Arrangement of Allegro Appassionato:

I've always had a keen interest in both classical and popular music, and the Allegro Appassionato by St. Saëns seemed like an ideal piece to combine these two styles. I began with a MIDI recording of the published piano reduction, and then added a drum track, electric bass, guitars, and other instruments to build the arrangement heard on this recording. All of the instrument sounds heard on this piece, except the solo cello, were created with synthesizers; however, the individual parts were performed in real time by my friends and me using a MIDI keyboard to play the notes. --Ethan Winer

Availability of Score and Parts:

You can purchase a nicely bound conductor's score for the cello concerto directly from Ethan Winer for $20 including postage within the US, or for $30 postpaid to other countries. A score and complete set of parts costs $75 including shipping or $85 foreign postpaid. This includes the score plus one each: Solo Cello, Piccolo, Flutes 1&2, Oboes, Clarinets 1&2, Bass Clarinet, Bassoons, Horns 1&2, Trumpets 1-3, Trombones 1-3, Tuba, Snare, Percussion, and Timpani; five copies Violin 1, five Violin 2, four Viola, four Cello, and three Bass. Additional parts are $3 each. All amounts are in US dollars.

Orders may be pre-paid by check, or charged to a Visa or Master Card credit card. Credit card orders may be placed by phone or email.

Ethan Winer
34 Cedar Vale Drive
New Milford, CT 06776 USA
860-350-8188
ethan@ethanwiner.com
www.ethanwiner.com

Music Minus One 'Cello

MMO

3716

Ethan Winer
Concerto for Cello & Orchestra in A minor

Franz Schubert
Ave Maria

Saint-Saëns
Allegro Appassionato

MMO Music Group • 50 Executive Boulevard, Elmsford, New York 10523, 1-(800) 669-7464
Website: www. minusone.com • E-mail: mmomus@aol.com